CONTENTS

Ravioli Quilts   3

Ravioli Blocks   4

Plaids 'n' Blues Ravioli Quilt   8

T-Shirt and Jeans Reverse Ravioli Quilt   11

Itsy Bits and Jeans Reverse Ravioli Quilt   13

T0364383

9781644036174

NOTE:

The slots in the template marking the 5˝ square were designed to be used with your water-erasable fabric markers and chalk pencils. If you are using something with a narrower tip, trace along either the inside or outside edge of the slot for consistency.

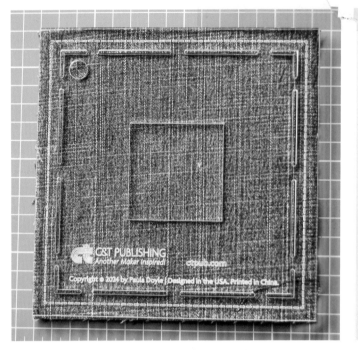

Text copyright © 2025 by Paula Doyle

Photography, and artwork copyright © 2025 by C&T Publishing, Inc.

Publisher: Amy Barrett-Daffin

Creative Director: Gailen Runge

Senior Editor: Roxane Cerda

Product Team: Betsy LaHonta, Gailen Runge

Cover/Book Designer: April Mostek

Production Coordinator: Tim Manibusan

Photography by Linda Seward, unless otherwise noted

Published by C&T Publishing, Inc., P.O. Box 1456, Lafayette, CA 94549

RAVIOLI QUILTS

Ravioli quilts are amazing!

- They are totally reversible.
- They use up leftover batting/wadding.
- They can be made any size.
- They quilt themselves... No more twisting or turning the quilt around and around while quilting.
- They can be made by absolute beginners or can even be taught to children!

Your 6″ × 6″ Ravioli Template

LINE A Use this slot to mark a 5″ × 5″ square onto the front and back of your main fabric. This will be your stitching line.

LINE B Mark this 2″ × 2″ square onto the center of your main fabric. This will help you position your accent fabric square.

LINE C Use this dashed line to help you trim your finished block.

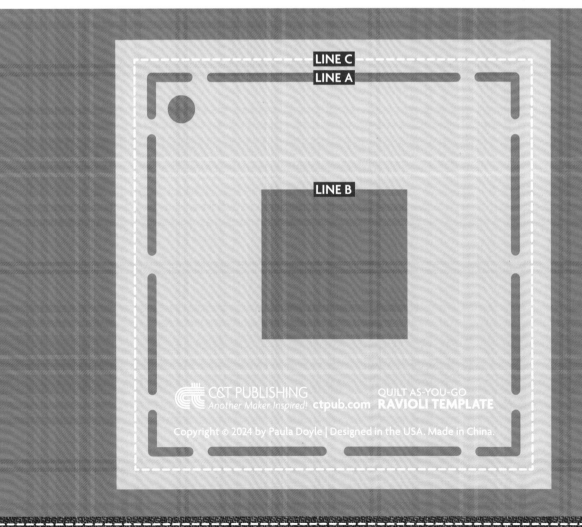

LINE C
LINE A
LINE B

C&T PUBLISHING
Another Maker Inspired! ctpub.com

QUILT AS-YOU-GO
RAVIOLI TEMPLATE

RAVIOLI BLOCKS

Block size: 5″ × 5″

MATERIALS AND SUPPLIES

For each Ravioli block, you will need:

- 1 square 6″ × 6″ primary fabric
- 1 square 6″ × 6″ backing fabric
- 1 square 4¾″ × 4¾″ batting
- 1 square 2½″ × 2½″ accent fabric, cut with a pinking blade or pinking shears

Other tools and supplies

- 45mm rotary cutter, equipped with a 45mm pinking blade and a 45mm plain blade
- fast2cut (R) Quilt As-You-Go Ravioli Template
- Removable marking pen or pencil that will show on your primary fabric
- Binding clips
- Sharp-pointed scissors
- Fabric glue stick
- Walking foot or even feed foot for your machine

Construction

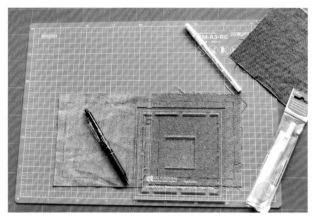

1. Cut the number of squares of your primary fabric (denim in these photos), backing fabric, accent fabric, and batting needed for your quilt.

2. Place the Ravioli template onto the right side of each square of primary fabric, lining up the corners, then use an erasable pen to mark in the dashed **line A** (which marks a centered 5″ × 5″ square) and solid **line B** (which marks a centered 2″ × 2″ square).

3. Turn the primary fabric square over, line up the ruler again, and mark **line A** onto the wrong side of the fabric.

4. Apply a bit of fabric glue just inside the corners of the 5″ × 5″ marked square on the wrong side of the primary fabric square, and glue the 4¾″ × 4¾″ piece of batting in place within the marked square.

6. Position the 2½″ × 2½″ pinked square of accent fabric over the marked 2″ × 2″ **line B** square on the front of the primary fabric square and hold it in place with a bit of fabric glue.

5. Position a 6″ × 6″ piece of backing fabric over the batting, wrong side toward the batting, creating a sandwich of primary fabric, batting, and backing squares. Match up the corners of the primary and backing fabric squares, and pin or secure each corner with a binding clip in preparation for sewing.

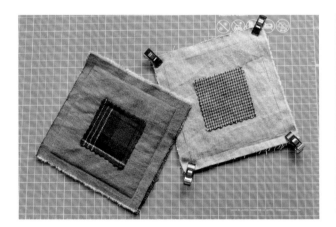

7. Stitch all around the 5″ × 5″ square **line A** marked on the right side of the primary fabric and ¼″ inside the outer edge of the 2½″ × 2½″ square with a straight stitch.

8. Stitch around the **line A** square and the center 2½″ × 2½″ square with a zigzag stitch on top of the straight stitch line. (Stitch length 1.0, stitch width 2.0). This zig zag stitching will ensure a minimal amount of fraying when the quilt is laundered!

9. Line up the white dashed **line C** over the line of the stitched seam, and trim each side of the 6″ × 6″ sandwich using the pinking blade in your rotary cutter. Once you trim each side of the sandwich, you will have a 5½″ × 5½″ Ravioli block. Make as many Ravioli blocks as you need to complete your quilt.

TIP: A slow and steady motion when cutting with the pinking blade is the best way to get a good clean cut!

10. Stitch the Ravioli blocks together into rows, using binding clips to secure the blocks while you stitch them together and a walking foot or an even feed foot and a size 80 or 90 needle. Stitch the blocks together from the primary fabric side, backing sides together, along the previously stitched seam lines.

11. Stitch rows of Ravioli blocks together, butting up the seam allowances at the corners, with top seam allowance pointed up, and bottom seam allowances downwards (so the feed dogs won't kick it up as you stitch). Once sewn together, each block will measure 5″ × 5″.

12. Using sharp pointed scissors, clip the seam allowances in the corners of the blocks where the fabrics are stitched down from sewing the rows together, allowing the seam allowances to be free. Shake the quilt out.

13. Bind your quilt and enjoy!

Accent Square Alternatives

USE QUILTING

Instead of using an accent square in the center of the block, free motion quilt inside the 2″ marked center squares.

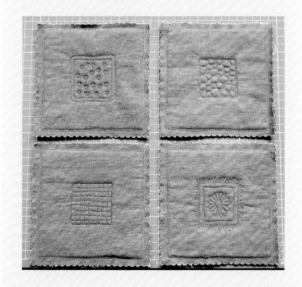

APPLIQUÉ FUN SHAPES

Fuse applique shapes in the center of the blocks and satin stitch around the edges. Fuse the shapes before layering your blocks and then satin stitch through all the layers in step 7 (page XX).

Different Size Ravioli Quilts

You can make your quilt any size, and any layout.

Cat/Dog Mat
20″ × 25″
20 blocks set 4 × 5

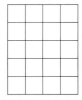

Playmat/Big Dog Mat
25″ × 35″
35 blocks set 5 × 7

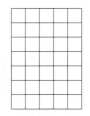

"Hug" Quilt
45″ × 65″
117 blocks set 9 × 13

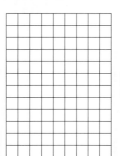

Sun or Beach Lounger
25″ × 75″
75 blocks set 5 × 15

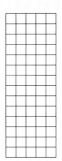

Sofa Quilt/Picnic Rug
65″ × 65″
139 blocks set 13 × 13

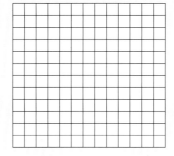

Care for your Ravioli Quilts

Wash Ravioli quilts by machine in warm water, using a mild detergent and no bleach. Tumble dry, then pull or snip off the threads as needed. Your washed RAVIOLI quilt will take on a soft fuzzy look with time!

PLAIDS 'N' BLUES RAVIOLI QUILT

Block size: 5″ × 5″ • **Quilt size:** 50″ × 75″ • **150 blocks set** 10 × 15

This is the coziest quilt you'll ever snuggle up to! Make your *Plaids 'n' Blues Ravioli Quilt* any size you desire, then simply let the raw edges on the denim side of the quilt fray! You may wash your finished quilt as many times as needed, just give the quilt a bit of a "haircut" after the first few washings.

MATERIALS AND SUPPLIES

For each Plaids 'n' Blues block you'll need:

- 1 square 6″ × 6″ blue denim
- 1 square 6″ × 6″ plaid flannel
- 1 square 4¾″ × 4¾″ batting
- 1 square 2½″ × 2½″ plaid flannel, cut with a pinking blade or pinking shears

See other tools and supplies (page 4).

Construction

1. Cut the number of squares in denim, flannel, and batting needed for your quilt.

2. Use the Ravioli template and fabric pen to mark the 5″ × 5″ square (**line A**) and 2″ × 2″ square (**line B**) on the right side of the denim square.

3. Tum the denim square over and use the template to mark the 5″ × 5″ square (**line A**) on the wrong side of the denim.

4. Apply a bit of the fabric glue just inside the corners of the 5″ × 5″ marked square on the wrong side of the denim square, and glue the 4¾″ × 4¾″ piece of batting in place within the marked square.

5. Position a 6″ × 6″ piece of flannel over the batting, wrong side toward the batting, creating a sandwich of denim, batting, and flannel squares. Match up the corners of the primary and backing fabric squares, and pin or secure each corner with a binding clip in preparation for sewing.

6. Position the 2½″ × 2½″ pinked flannel square over the marked 2″ × 2″ **line B** square on the front of the denim square and hold it in place with a bit of the fabric glue.

7. Stitch all around the 5″ × 5″ square **line A** marked on the right side of the denim and ¼″ inside the outer edge of the 2½″ × 2½″ flannel square with a straight stitch.

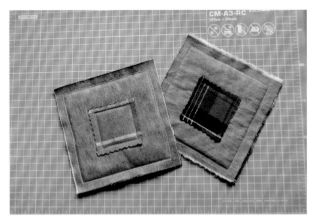

8. Stitch around the **line A** square with a zigzag stitch (on top of the straight stitch line).

9. Line up the white dashed **line C** over the line of the stitched seam, and trim each side of the 6″ × 6″ block using the pinking blade in your rotary cutter. Once you trim each side of the sandwich, you will have a 5½″ × 5½″ Ravioli block. Make as many Ravioli blocks as you need to complete your quilt.

10. Sew the blocks into rows, flannel sides of the block together.

11. Sew the rows together, flannel sides together.

12. Using sharp pointed scissors, clip the seam allowances in the corners of the blocks where the fabrics are stitched down from sewing the rows together, allowing the seam allowances to be free. Shake the quilt out.

13. Bind your quilt and enjoy!

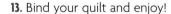
Finished quilt

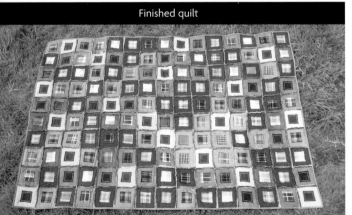

T-SHIRT AND JEANS REVERSE RAVIOLI QUILT

Block size: 5″ × 5″ • Quilt size: 25″ × 75″ • 75 blocks set 5 × 15

For this version of the Ravioli quilt, you will use up your favorite old t-shirts as well as your jeans! Here it has been made into a quilt for a sun lounger, or to place on the ground or sand, jeans side down. The fabric from the t-shirts is simply treated with spray starch (I recommend Terial Magic) to make it easier to cut and use.

MATERIALS AND SUPPLIES

For each T-Shirt and Jeans block you'll need:

- 1 square 6″ × 6″ denim
- 1 square 6″ × 6″ t-shirt fabric*
- 1 square 4¾″ × 4¾″ batting
- 1 appliqué for the center of the block made from T-shirt fabric, backed with fusible web (this can be any shape) See other tools and supplies (page 4).

* Before cutting, apply spray starch to the t-shirt fabric, let it soak in, then iron flat.

Construction

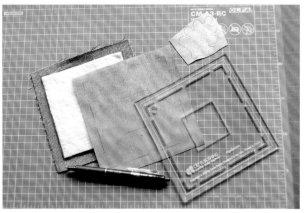

1. Use the Ravioli template and fabric pen to mark the 5″ × 5″ square (**line A**) on both sides of your t-shirt fabric.

2. Fuse the appliqué shape in place in the center of the t-shirt square.

3. Use a little bit of fabric glue to stick the 4¾″ × 4¾″ piece of batting in place within the marked square on the wrong side of the t-shirt square.

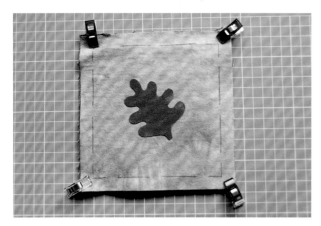

4. Place a denim square on top, wrong side toward the batting, creating a sandwich of t-shirt fabric, batting, and denim squares.

5. Stitch all around the 5″ × 5″ square **line A** marked on the right side of the t-shirt fabric.

6. Zigzag stitch around the square on top of the line of straight stitches and free motion quilt or satin stitch around the edges of the applique piece.

7. Refer to steps 9–13 on page 6 to finish the quilt.

Finished squares

ITSY BITS AND JEANS REVERSE RAVIOLI QUILT

Block size: 5″ × 5″ • **Quilt size:** 60″ × 60″ • 144 blocks set 12 × 12

This version of the Ravioli quilt uses up scraps of leftover fabrics from other quilting projects and old jeans, plus a little decorative stitching!

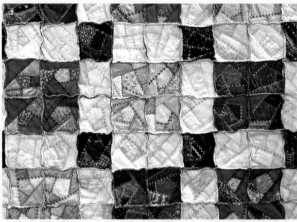

Itsy Bits blocks

Denim side

MATERIALS AND SUPPLIES

For each Itsy Bits and Jeans block, you will use:

- 1 square 6″ × 6″ denim
- 1 square 4¾″ × 4¾″ batting
- Several Itsy Bits, which are leftover pieces of patchwork fabric measuring approximately 3″ × 3″

See other tools and supplies (page 4).

Construction

1. Use the Ravioli template and fabric pen to mark the 5″ × 5″ square (**line A**) on both sides of the denim square.

2. Use a little bit of fabric glue to stick the 4¾″ × 4¾″ piece of batting in place within the marked square on the wrong side of the denim square.

3. Position the central Itsy Bit of fabric onto the batting.

4. Stitch a 2nd Itsy Bit onto the first Itsy Bit (right sides together) and finger press the seam.

5. Continue with a 3rd Itsy Bit and so on until the block is covered.

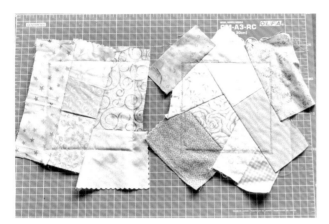

6. Flip the block over and stitch around the marked line from the denim side with a straight stitch and then a zigzag stitch.

7. From the front of the block, Sew decorative stitches over the seam lines.

Finished squares

8. Refer to steps 9–13 on page 6 to finish the quilt.

ABOUT THE AUTHOR

Despite being born in Massachusetts, Paula Doyle was raised in Brazil, the daughter of Methodist missionary teachers. Paula's mother taught her how to use a sewing machine at the age of nine. At the age of ten, she made her first patchwork cushion under the instruction of her maternal grandmother.

After a career in banking in California, Paula moved to London in 1987 and married Mark Doyle. During a subsequent seven-year overseas posting to the United States and Canada, quilting became a passion for Paula after she made her first sampler quilt in a class at La Maison de Calico, a quilt shop in Pointe-Claire, Quebec, in 1991.

Photo by Geoffrey Rippingale

Paula and Mark then moved to Connecticut. Paula started to teach patchwork and quilting at the local YWCA, at the local quilt guild, and even to a group of nuns in a monastery. Returning to England in 1995, Paula opened Green Mountain Quilt Shop, where she continued to teach quilting classes and started designing her own quilts and quilt patterns. After thirteen years in business, Paula closed the shop in 2008 and decided to concentrate on designing quilts and quilt patterns in her home garden studio. Her emphasis is on simplifying techniques that make complex-looking quilts achievable and fun for all levels of quilters.

Paula is the author of *Easy Stack Quilts* and *Mini-Mosaic Quilts* (both by C&T Publishing); she has also published many of her patterns in quilt magazines. In 2014, Paula brought together a group of local quilters, the Magna Carta Quilt Association, to make Magna Carta quilts in celebration of the 800-year anniversary of the sealing of the Magna Carta at nearby Runnymede. The quilts were finished and exhibited at the Great Charter Festival at the Royal Holloway University of London in June 2015 and then displayed at Guildford Cathedral before traveling to the U.S. to be exhibited in Houston and Chicago.

Follow Paula on Social Media:

Website
greenmountainquilts.com

Facebook
Green Mountain Quilt Studio

Instagram
@greenmountainquilter

See Paula's Youtube video for more information